Curve
Economics

Curve Economics

To Ross,
I hope you enjoy
reading my first book.
From your first
Geospatial commission
'coach' ?
Asad

Asad Ghani

About the author

Asad Ghani has been a professional economist for over a decade. He holds a master's degree in economics from the London School of Economics and has taught micro-economics at the undergraduate level at Queen Mary University of London. *Curve Economics* is his first book.

Acknowledgements

would like to thank Joe Betts, Laurissa Miles, Kim Wager and David Marshall for their support whilst I was writing this book.

Contents

About this book

This book applies an economic framework to a collection of personal anecdotes in a humorous and engaging way.

Economics is often described as the social science that studies the scarcity of resources. For me, it's a glorious subject that I've studied for 15 years. I quickly realised that economics can be applied to almost any real-life event. Also, I believe that good economics should be explained in a concise and simple manner.

I have a passion for visual techniques that support the understanding of economics. This book contains 35 real short stories accompanied by a chart or equation to help describe the economics they illustrate.

I hope you enjoy reading about my trading days in nursery, how frugal I am with money and how an office stapler can cripple productivity.

#1

Law of diminishing returns

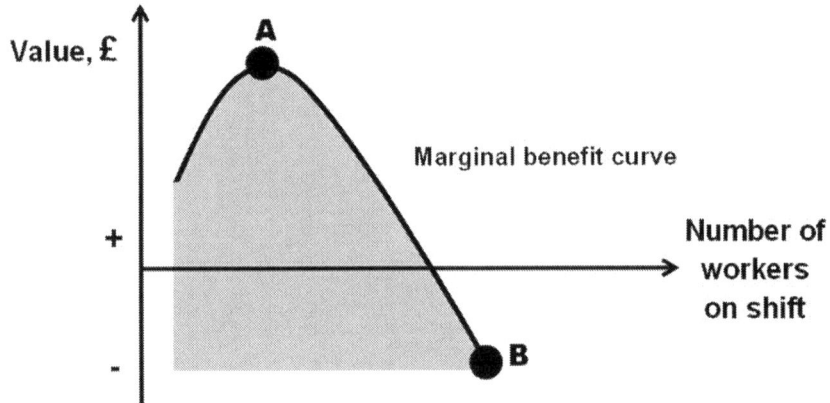

E veryone remembers his or her first paid job, and I vividly recall mine, as it lasted for three complete days (including one day of health and safety training) before I was dismissed. My untimely exit was all due to the law of diminishing returns. I remember it as if it were yesterday: I was a chubby teenager excited to start earning my own cash at a newly opened coffee shop in my local town centre. Little did I know that a social science called economics would scupper my summer job.

The recruiting manager decided to hire a gazillion or so staff for a small coffee shop outlet. After going through barista training class 101, we embarked on our first shift serving live customers. We started our shifts in half-hour intervals, and after a few hours of trading, each extra staff member that joined found productive tasks to carry out. The coffee machine was manned up, the ovens were spewing out hot muffins and our panini were flying off the shelves. In economics talk, each extra staff member added a little extra marginal benefit. We had hit point A.

Then, enter more staff just before lunchtime, ramping up to full staff on shift for that day. Things went sour quite quickly after that. We ended up with an over-staffed production set-up in which it was difficult to move sideways without stepping on someone's toes. The marginal benefit (the extra output from an extra shift worker) fell to the extent that we reached the dreaded point B.

Point B was a dire place to be, as we would have been better off without the last few eager souls that came on shift (they actually slowed down service and restricted sales).

Finally, when my manager added up the day's takings and looked at our salary bill, she issued my P45 quicker than I could pull a shot of espresso. In dismissing me (along with a few others), my manager reduced the number of staff on shift to a point at which the benefit extra workers added would equal the cost of employing them!

The J curve

For some people, the thought of undergoing a workplace change in IT systems would rank on a par with sticking pins in their eyes in terms of personal enjoyment. I suffer from technology phobia, and owning a Nintendo DS is about as flash as it gets in terms of my IT capacity. So, the day my employer announced that we would be moving from fixed desk computers to laptops sent a cold shudder down my spine. The IT team installing a program called FileZilla (a more appropriate name for Godzilla's wife) on my laptop to accommodate the changes didn't reassure me.

On transition day, like an army boot camp, all staff were issued a laptop, a power lead and a laptop sleeve, along with a deluge of new passwords. This boot camp session involved logging onto things and other IT alchemy beyond my comprehension. The amount of work produced by the office fell dramatically overnight. Even on day two, inevitable problems with server connections and lack of familiarity with a whizzier operating system slowed our productivity.

Had the decision to move to laptops been a complete disaster? The resounding answer is no! In the coming weeks, the servers cooled down (or whatever they do to actually work), we all learned the new software and we were back to normal productivity. After that, we utilised the flexibility of being able to 'pow wow' in open office spaces to work collaboratively. And, in a rather disturbing stalking style, we could track each other's login activity and whereabouts (without the need for tags on our ankles). The better software, faster connections and freedom to work anywhere increased our productivity and overall output. In economics, we had moved along the J curve.

NB: The J curve is named as such because the curve looks like the letter J, where there is an initial deterioration followed by an improvement beyond the starting level.

The secretary problem

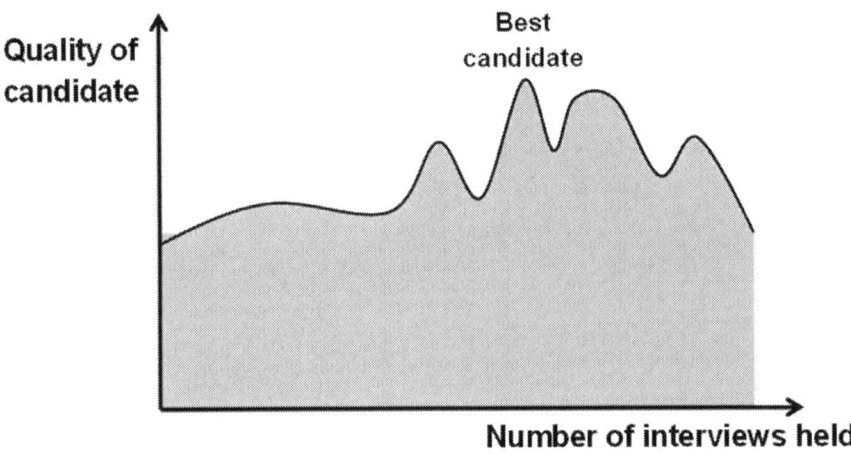

Quality of candidate

Best candidate

Number of interviews held

T he 'secretary problem' has never been an issue for me, as I've always been too junior to have a secretary. The thought of a person who sets up my meetings, prints out my papers and makes the occasional cup of coffee would actually be a blessing. The rather cryptic title refers to the problem of when to stop interviewing candidates for a job vacancy.

Several times, I've had the unhappy pleasure of sifting through job hopefuls, and the application stage reveals a mix of characters. Time is precious and a decision needs to be made on how many people should be interviewed. Too few interviews, and you risk hiring a mediocre person from a small field, bust the playing field wide open and interview every Tom, Dick and Sally, and your valuable time is monopolised. The only plus side is replenishing your cache of intriguing dinner party tales of bizarre competency-based answers from the odder candidates. Well, the law of large numbers means the extreme outliers are likely to make an appearance!

My years of being on interview panels have led me to conclude that the optimal answer is always to interview a handful of people (after sifting through them first). However, I stumbled on a rather simple and ingenious mathematical formula that offers an alternative approach. The solution to this quandary is to always reject the first (n/e) candidates interviewed, where n is the number of applicants and e is the base of the natural logarithm. You then carry on interviewing and stop at the point when the last interviewee was better than all of the interviewees before him or her. Working through this rocket science-level maths means that the probability of selecting the best candidate with this approach is 1/e, which is about 37%. The next challenge is to convince human resource departments of this formula! I'll leave it to you to think of a fair way to assign interview slots. My best idea thus far is to make candidates draw straws.

NB: e is an important and well-known number in mathematics. In addition to being the base of the natural logarithm, it is an irrational number, like pi (π), so it has unlimited decimal places. To three decimal places, e is equal to 2.718.

The backward-bending labour supply curve

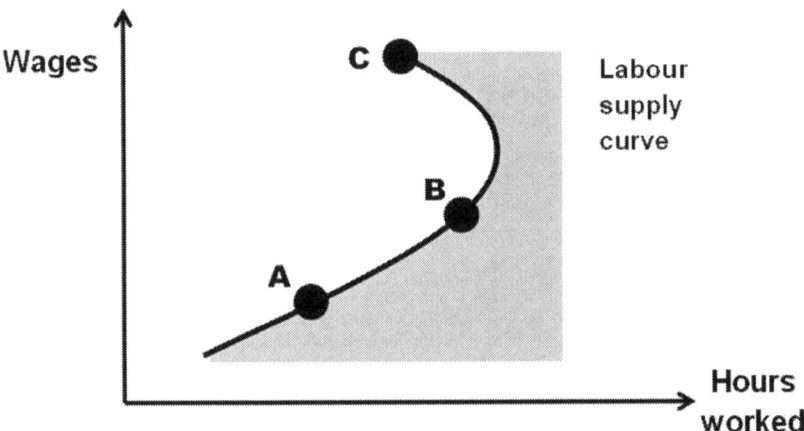

My field of specialisation is labour economics, so it's only natural to include the backward-bending labour supply curve in this book. This humble curve charts my career progression from my naive days as a young graduate right up to the dizzying heights of my current position as a senior economist.

In 2003, I was a baby-faced graduate starting my first office job. My wages were around £13 per hour, and I worked 37 hours per week. I had no idea how to log on to desk telephones or how to use a fax machine. A few years later, I had established myself as an experienced graduate employee. My salary increased incrementally along with my working hours, which grew to 40 hours per week at an hourly wage of £15 (point A). A 40-hour week coincided nicely with me arriving five minutes before my boss and leaving five minutes after he left. My lucky promotion break happened on April Fools' Day in 2008. My working hours took another hike: a whopping 46 hours per week at £20 per hour (point B). The laws of economics were operating to a tee. As my wages increased, so did the number of hours I worked – an upward-sloping labour supply curve.

In 2013, I was promoted yet again, and my salary peaked at an amazing £30 per hour, yet my hours worked per week fell (point C). Why hadn't my hours worked increased again? In economics, the income effect had begun to dominate the substitution effect.

The substitution effect refers to the fact that as my wages increase, the opportunity cost of enjoying my leisure increases. For example, if I decide to work less and enjoy a leisurely stroll in the park, the cost of the stroll increases (in terms of wages foregone). This substitution effect encourages me to work more as my wages increase.

On the other hand, the income effect means that I can earn the same amount of wages by working fewer hours if my hourly wage increases. The income effect entices me to work fewer hours. When my hours fell back, the income effect dominated the substitution effect, and after years of slogging away in junior job roles, thank goodness for the income effect in my senior roles. Maybe this explains the wider phenomenon of why bosses seem to work fewer hours than their staff?

Production possibility frontier

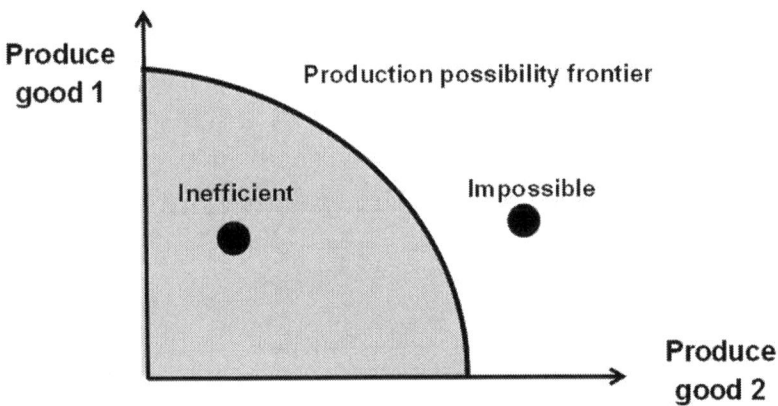

It's amazing how the modest stapler can introduce mass ineffi-ciency in an office. Its primary purpose is to bind sheets of paper together, yet it can cripple office output in an instant. Where I work, finding a stapler is like striking gold. We start the year with enough staplers to go around, and then somehow, they magically start to disappear. As far as I'm aware, none of my colleagues at-tended Hogwarts, so alternate theories for the disappearances are rife. If you are lucky enough to find a stapler, it usually starts deterio-rating in effectiveness quicker than an England cricket team batting collapse. After just a few uses, the inevitable stapler jam rears its ugly head.

In economics, output is often produced using both capital and labour. Capital in my office consists of my laptop, the printers, the office building, etc. Included in this list is the modest stapler. At work, I can divide my output into two main groups: economic reports and policy projects. Due to the scarcity of working staplers, I find my precious time is often wasted searching for a working one, or it is wasted banging a jammed stapler against my desk. The old desk-bashing technique is the best way to dislodge pesky staples that get stuck. In economics terms, I am operating within the production possibility frontier (PPF). The PPF is a curve that plots out the maximum amount of output that I can produce if I use all of my resources efficiently. In my case, I'm producing less economic reports and policy projects given my resources due to stapler issues (point inefficient). On a good day and with effective capital inputs, I fly through work. I can produce reports and work on projects that maximise my output on the PPF curve. This is despite when I'm impossibly tasked with drafting one hundred reports in a week, which is beyond the output that I can produce within my resources. This point is appropriately named the impossible point and lies outside the PPF curve.

During one lunch break, after being driven to despair by my broken stapler, I decided to invest in my own effective capital stock. I nipped down to Paperchase and purchased a sleek, frosted stapler. The efficient clicking sound as my papers were bound together was music to my ears. No more would I have to sift through random unattached pieces of paper, and I was back up to maximum output. Having also purchased the only frosted stapler in the office, this kept the magicians from performing any of their disappearing acts as well!

Normal distribution

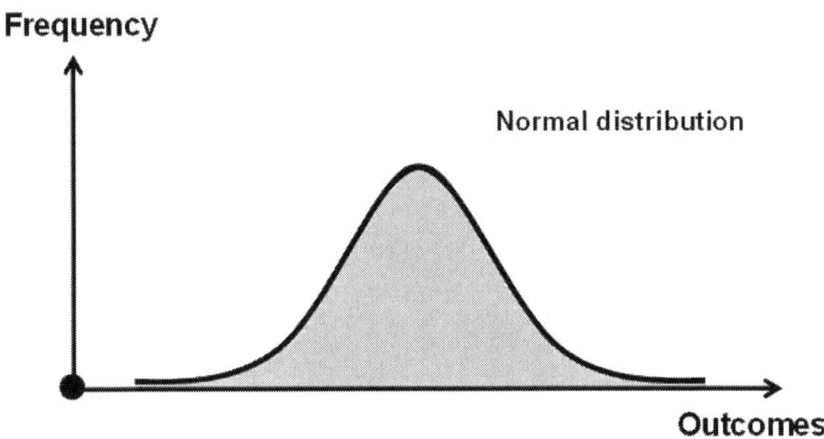

Frequency

Normal distribution

Outcomes

I n May 2015, I sat possibly the hardest exam that I've ever encountered. It surpassed my A-level physics exams, my undergraduate economics exams, my master's economics exams and
even my driving theory test! What was this mentally gruelling exam?
It was the Mensa administered intelligence quotient (IQ) test. For
those who have never heard of Mensa, it's a high IQ society. The
only entry requirement is being in the top 2% of IQ scores (the tech-
nical term is being 'gifted').

IQ scores are thought to be normally distributed. In plain English, there are a few people with very low IQs, then gradually, more people with higher IQs. This is followed by a huge mass of people of average intelligence, and then gradually, fewer people who are brighter than average. After that, there are only a few individuals who are the very brightest, or 'the gifted'.

When plotted, the normal distribution takes the shape of a bell. My motives for taking the Mensa exam were partly fuelled by curiosity and partly due to the interesting promotional material on their website. One genius on the members' page said that joining Mensa introduced her to the complex world of ordering meals at Nando's!

Like Daniel La Russo (the karate kid), I prepared using slightly unorthodox training. It didn't quite involve wax on wax off, but it did involve hours of Sudoku-type puzzle-solving.

Mensa allows candidates to sit two tests, and a score that is high enough to be in the top 2% in either test opens the doors to Mensa. I sat my tests at my old undergraduate university and relished the challenge. With pen in hand, I entered the exam room. What would my fellow exam-takers be like? In short (literally and figuratively), they were ten 12-year-old children! I knew Mensa was a genius-type society, but I wasn't expecting a field of contenders who still thought a Happy Meal was good value for money.

The tests lasted for over one hour. It was like taking part in The Crystal Maze and being selected to complete a mental challenge again and again. A few weeks later, I got my results. Had I managed to sneak into the far right corner of the normal distribution of IQ scores? My results placed me in the top 3%, which is analogous to waiting for hours at a theme park ride and reaching the front of the queue only to be told the ride was closing.

Type 1 or type 2 error?

		Hypothesis (H_0)	
		True	False
Judgement	Reject	Type 1 error	Correct
	Accept	Correct	Type 2 error

It was the summer of 2006 and the FIFA world cup was being hosted in Germany. With a one-hour time zone difference and multiple fixtures per day, its effect on staff's presence during office hours was tangible. My senior boss revealed his misjudgement when he called my own impeccable allegiance into question.

I remember this day in some detail. I had toddled off to a research meeting with my line manager and external consultants. The meeting organiser had conveniently scheduled the meeting to coincide with the Germany versus Argentina knockout game in the afternoon. I mean, how many times do you actually get to watch high-calibre fixtures in the world cup? For the majority of world cup tournaments, the piglets are hogging the group phase matches, so the knock-out stage matches are to be savoured.

Diligently and professionally, I attended the meeting and gave it my all. I returned to my desk near the end of the day, ready to clock off and enjoy the second half of the game in the pub, when my senior manager unburdened his guilty conscience: he thought I was already at the pub watching the game. How mistaken he was! My senior manager had made what is called in economics a type two error.

Economists love to create hypotheses to test. My senior manager had constructed a hypothesis in his head that I had buggered off to watch the game. This is referred to as the null hypothesis in economics, denoted by H_0. This was false, but he accepted his own judgement. It was when I returned to my desk that he realised his error. Had I actually been watching the game while he thought I was at the meeting, he would have made a type one error.

I managed to catch the second half of the game, which resulted in a mass brawl between the German and Argentinian players at the final whistle. The animal instincts of the pub-goers came to the fore as they egged the players on (despite being thousands of miles away and on the other side of a TV screen).

What I learnt from this episode is that even my senior manager, who I held in high regard, was susceptible to type two errors. This is unfortunate for me, as I would definitely prefer that he make type one errors instead!

#8

Bargaining game

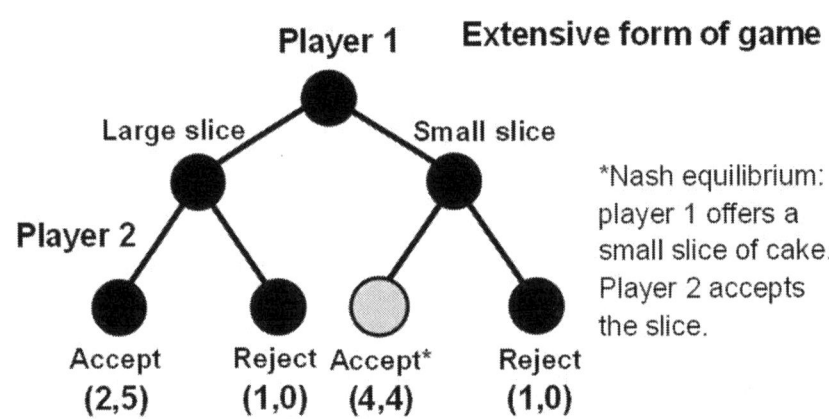

Player 1   **Extensive form of game**

Large slice   Small slice

Player 2

*Nash equilibrium:
player 1 offers a
small slice of cake.
Player 2 accepts
the slice.

Accept   Reject   Accept*   Reject
(2,5)   (1,0)   (4,4)   (1,0)

At work, I am notorious for eating an entire cake at my desk on an almost daily basis. It's a surprise that I've delayed the inevitable onset of diabetes for so long! Occasionally, I share a slice of my cake and ask for a favour in return. To the unknowing recipient, he or she is taking part in a bargaining game. The famous mathematician John Nash (played by Russell Crowe in the film *A Beautiful Mind*) was a major contributor to game theory.

According to Nash, the best way to play a game is to pick your best response given the action of the other player. In my cake-sharing situation, I'm player one, and the work colleague from whom I want help (in exchange for a slice of cake) is player two. I've got the option to be stingy and offer a small slice of cake or to be incredibly generous by giving away a large slice. Now, player two can either accept my slice offer, eat some delicious cake and help me, or player two can reject my offer, not help me and end up cake-less.

What's the best thing for me to do? Well, I like cake, but I also need my colleague's help. The solution to this problem comes from analysing the payoffs from the four possible outcomes. Let's start with my colleague being unhelpful and rejecting my offer of cake irrespective of the size of the slice. In payoff terms, neither my colleague nor myself are happy, as I don't get any help and he or she gets no yummy cake. This is represented in the diagram as the numbers in the brackets (1,0). The first number is my payoff value, and the second number is my colleague's payoff. I've got a positive number, as I've got more cake to eat. My colleague gets zero, as nothing changes for him or her.

Looking at the payoffs available for my colleague and I, we will both be better off in the decision branches where my offer of cake is accepted. Now, assuming that I'm aware of this, what size slice should I offer? A no-brainer at this point is that it must be a small slice. This is because my colleague likes my chocolate fudge cake, so he or she considers that eating some (even a small slice) is better than not eating any. I like cake, so if I can offer my colleague a small slice and still get help in exchange, I'll take that option. The Nash equilibrium in this game is for me to offer a small slice of cake in exchange for help and for that offer to be accepted. I have played this game using chocolate fudge, coffee and walnut, salted caramel and carrot cake, and the outcome is always the same.

The penalty taker

Normal form of game

Penalty taker (Player 1)

*Best response

		Left	Right
Goalkeeper **(Player 2)**	Left	Save (0,1*)	Goal (1*,0)
	Right	Goal (1*,0)	Save (0,1*)

No game is more beautiful than football, so it's fitting that economic game theory can be applied to penalty kicks. Growing up, I was never good at sports, but I enthusiastically organised a five-a-side football league at work. During my doomed primary school days, I was relegated to the green house team. A better name would have been the loser house, as we always finished last on sports day. My luck didn't change as an adult – the football team I played for wasn't much better.

As captain of my football team, the important responsibility of taking penalties fell on my shoulders. On one occasion, there was a long delay before I took a penalty. During this period, I changed my mind about shooting left or right again and again. By the time I approached the penalty spot, I had fully confused myself and ended up gently rolling the ball forward. The goalkeeper made an easy save by sitting on top of the ball to stop it trickling over the goal line. What was the best strategy? Should I have shot to the left or to the right?

An intuitive answer can be set out using game theory. I can be considered as player one, the penalty taker who can shoot left or right. The goalkeeper is player two and can dive left or right. Payoffs are again represented in brackets, with player one's payoff the first number and player two's the second number.

If the goalkeeper dives left, I should of course shoot right and vice versa to score a goal (we are assuming that I hit the target). From the goalkeeper's perspective, his or her best response to me shooting right is to dive right to save the ball. Similarly, the goalkeeper should dive left if I shoot left. A Nash equilibrium occurs if both players pick their best response given the other player's action (these are denoted by asterisks). As can be seen, there are no situations in which both players are choosing a best response.

What is the solution? In economics, I must apply a mixed strategy of sometimes shooting left and sometimes shooting right. If I do this, sometimes the ball will be saved, but on other occasions, I can bask in the glory of scoring a goal (providing I don't completely scuff my shot).

Laffer curve

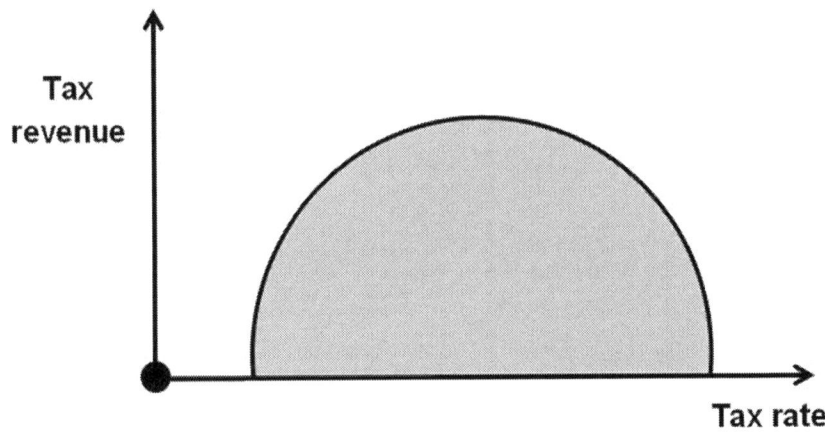

Tax revenue

Tax rate

We have a tea club system at work. This club was set up for the greater good of our team so that we could avoid frittering away money on expensive shop-bought chai tea lattes or English breakfast tea. The club runs on the basis of collecting a £3 monthly membership fee, which then allows us unlimited access to milk, PG tips and Douwe Egbert's coffee.

The £3 fee can be considered as a type of lump sum tax. Taxation is one method governments use to raise income to fund public services. In our situation, the tea club tax is the mechanism to raise money to fund the supplies offered in the tea club. But what is the ideal rate to set for this tax? Two main factors will drive this decision.

First, the caffeine dependency of the office will determine the demand for tea club supplies. Given that tea and coffee demand is high in my office, the success of the club depends on the fridge and cupboards being adequately stocked. The second factor is therefore picking a tax rate that maximises tax revenue so that a lot of supplies can be bought.

The relationship between tax revenue and tax rates is set out in the famous Laffer curve. The curve looks like a concave function. As a reminder, a concave function forms a semi-circle: it rises, reaches a zenith and then falls back. The logic behind this relationship is simple. A tax rate of zero yields no tax revenue. A rate higher than zero results in positive tax revenues. But at some point, the tax rates become too expensive. This leads to tax evasion (people stealing milk from the fridge). Alternatively, people could completely withdraw from the tea club. Both of these outcomes lead to a reduction in total tax revenues.

Judging by the longevity of the tea club, its high membership, a well-stocked fridge and cupboards and the recent luxurious move to Douwe Egbert's coffee, I would bet that £3 is near a tax rate that maximises the tea club's revenues.

Location problem

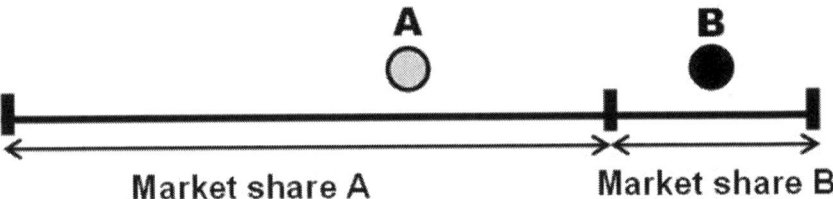

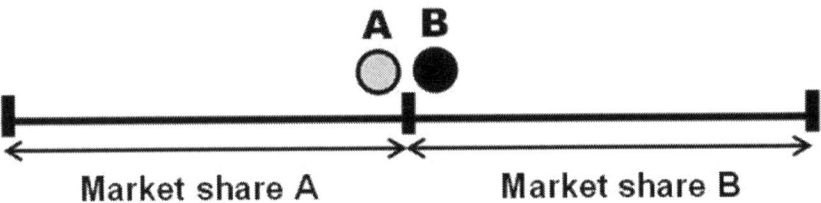

'm fortunate to work near a wonderful food market in London where I can buy dishes from all areas of the globe. I've become accustomed to the excellent falafel, tandoori meats and roasted chicken on offer. It's convenient to buy lunch there, as it's close to my office and it allows me to stretch my legs at lunchtime. The popularity of the cuisine on offer has led to a growth in the number of stalls from two to eight.

Initially, the two stalls were quite some distance apart. Over time, they congregated toward the middle of the road. Why were the stall-holders moving toward each other? What was unfolding was the economics location problem.

The food offered at all the stalls would pass the Gordon Ramsey kitchen nightmares benchmark (i.e. each stall has damned good food). Combine this with fairly lazy people (or time-poor people), and customers will be heavily inclined to buy their lunch from the first stall they encounter.

Customers coming from the top of the road will go to stall A, and customers who enter from the bottom of the road will purchase lunch from stall B. Customers who find themselves between the stalls are likely to purchase from the nearest stall. With this dynamic in play, it doesn't make sense for both stalls to be located anywhere else but the middle of the street. If they did have a different location, there would always be an incentive for one stall-holder to edge closer to the other to gain a larger share of the customers.

This dynamic cannot last if more stall-holders enter the food market (which they did). If people still bought from the nearest stall, it would make sense to set up trade further away from the rest of the market. Not to mention that a mass congregation in the middle of the road would cause a logistical calamity. To simplify things, the break-away market trader would get the bulk of business from people who approach from the top (or bottom) of the street.

The movement of the market stalls was the equilibrium solution unfolding before my very eyes: any inconvenience that I felt from the stalls relocating paled in comparison to the supermarkets that constantly changed the location of where my teabags could be found.

Complements

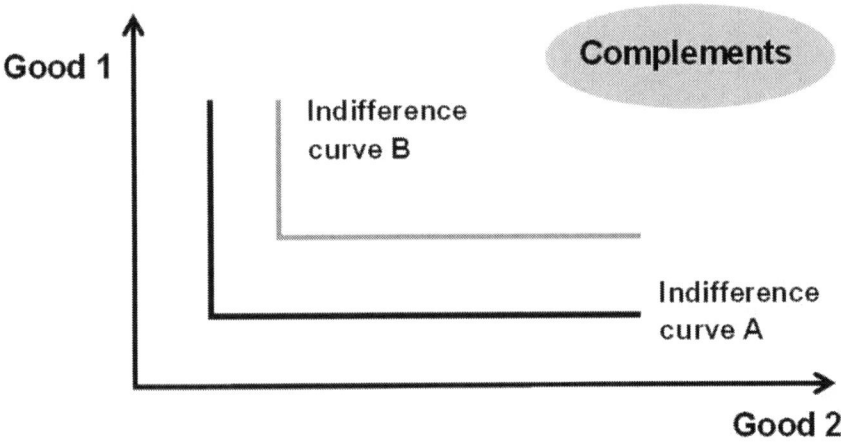

The word compliment can be used in the sentence 'your hair looks nice', or, if spelt 'complement', it would be more appropriate in 'the house red wine complements the beef steak'. This tale of economics focuses on the latter context, but in my case, baked beans best complement my chips.

As an impoverished young graduate, my lunchtime diet would consist of a £1.30 portion of chips and beans. It's a testament to my strong preference for chips with beans that I ate this meal for an amazing 180 lunches in a row. In economics, complements describe goods or services that are consumed together, usually in fixed proportions.

My enjoyment of my poor man's lunch would be heavily dependent on the right proportion of chips to beans. Too many beans and there wouldn't be enough chips to soak up the succulent tomato juice. Too many chips and I ran the risk of eating a lonely bunch of dry chips at the end of the meal. How can this relationship best be described on a chart?

The answer is through the use of L-shaped indifference curves. Indifference curves plot all the combinations of chips and beans that leave me with the same level of utility (a posh economics word for enjoyment). The L shape comes from the fact that I like chips and beans served in the right proportions. Too much of either good (without the other) doesn't actually make me any happier – it just leaves me indifferent.

In the canteen that I frequented, this wasn't much of a problem. The server tended to sweat a lot behind the hot counter, and he would use his spoon to count out canteen proportions with freakish accuracy. The only problem with this was the nervousness that built as I waited in the queue – I didn't want to get the lunch serving with extra sweat added in. This was a real and present danger, as droplets of sweat had a tendency to drip off of his nose!

But what if I got more of both chips and beans if someone else served me? If the proportions met my meticulous demands, this would give me extra enjoyment and move me onto a higher indifference curve. Be warned, this would stop at some point, as I've only got so much space in my stomach to store this heavenly combination.

Edgeworth box

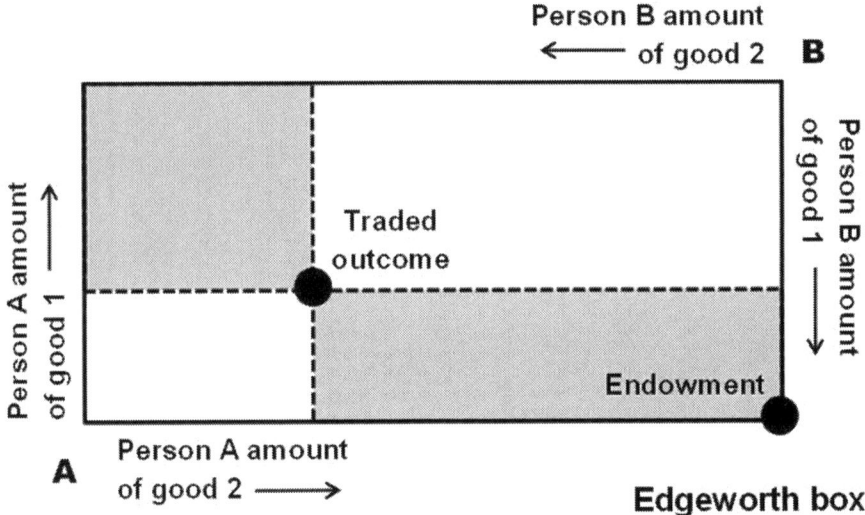

Edgeworth box

I dabbled in the economics of trade from an early age without even knowing it. At four and a half years old, I started nursery. I was a scrawny kid who cried like hell on my first day. I remember the tears flowing on my inaugural day. The teacher handed me a blue paper towel that had the softness of fine-grade sandpaper to wipe away my tears. Funnily enough, I never cried at nursery again after that day.

After adjusting to the shock of having to turn up to a fixed place at a fixed time on weekdays and not being allowed to bring my tricycle along, I settled in. The routine became familiar, along with the concept of trading with the other children. Our best trading market was at lunchtime, where we could devise a bartering type economy without the need for any currency. Our market information was almost perfect, as we would all sit in a circle on the rug offering out rates of exchange for our lunch items. All we needed were bright-coloured jackets and hand signals, and it would have been like a stock exchange trading floor.

When goods are exchanged, the Edgeworth box forms a neat graphical representation between two parties. The rectangular box indicates the amounts of good 1 and good 2 that each party has to start off with. This point is called the endowment point. In the diagram above, the endowment point shows person A having all of good 2 and person B having all of good 1.

The traded outcome at nursery would usually start off with this type of endowment. Good 1 and 2 would depend on the shopping habits of your parents. In my case, I was lucky enough to have icing sugar biscuits. Other children demanded them, as their cupboards at home didn't stock any of these sweet delights. I needed to trade, as the other component of my lunch was a plain, heavily buttered sandwich.

At the end of lunchtime, we would end up with traded outcomes in which most kids had some of good 1 and some of good 2. Looking back at my nursery days, it's amazing that economics can even be applied to a bunch of innocent four year olds.

#14

Comparative advantage

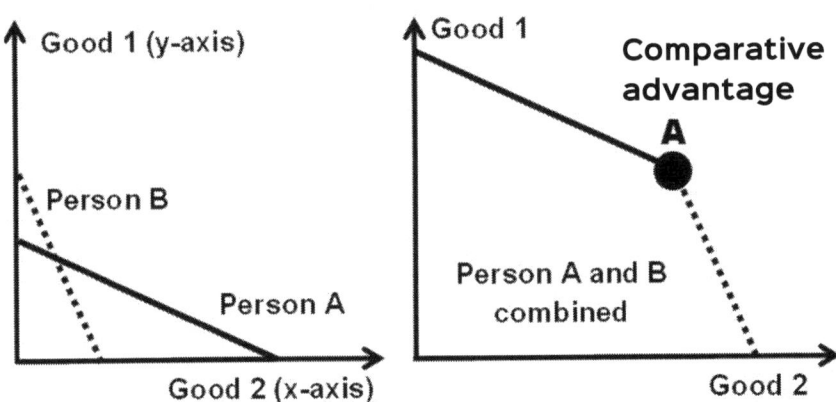

Nobody in life is perfect – we all have different strengths and weaknesses. Well, that's what I tend to say after playing football, which, as you know, I'm hopeless at. In an office environment, I work with other types of analysts, including statisticians. My professional analyst discipline is economics. In these instances, I'm more knowledgeable about economics compared to my statistician colleagues –I have a distinct comparative advantage over them when it comes to economics. The tables are turned when it comes to statistics; which is their forte compared to mine.

Is there a way of representing this on a graph? Economics is notorious for boiling things down to simple models, and the concept of comparative advantage can be plotted on a modest two-plane graph. The graph features two goods that are produced: good 1 and good 2. The economy being examined has two people: person A and person B. In my case, the two goods could represent statistical analysis (good 1) and economic analysis (good 2). The two people under consideration are myself (the economist, person A) and the statistician (person B).

The first graph shows that if person B, the statistician, only produced statistical work, he or she would produce more than me. This point is on the y-axis. If we look at the x-axis, I can produce more economic reports than the statistician if I focus entirely on producing economic analysis. In reality, both types of analysts could produce a mixture of both statistical work and economic analysis. The line that connects the points on the boundary y-axis and x-axis represents this.

The steepness of the line indicates where the comparative advantage in production is. Given that good 1 here is representing statistics, a very steep line indicates a better statistician compared to economist. A flatter line indicates a better economist than statistician, if the yardstick we are using is producing output. Combining both lines for person A and person B (if they worked as a team) gives the joint production set. These are all of the possible production combinations of statistics and economics that the team can produce. What is usually observed is specialisation (point A): the statistician ends up producing all of the stats and the economist focuses on economics. This seems plausible, and it is the reasoning I use on my graduate statisticians when I don't want to spend hours laboriously extracting data.

Critical mass

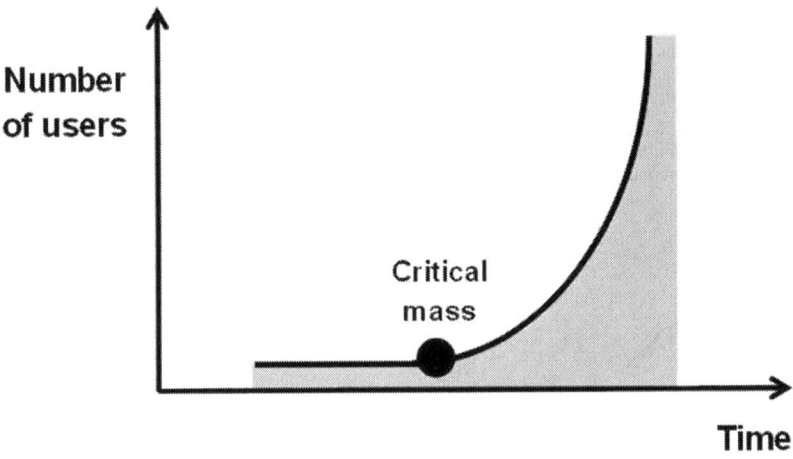

Some things in life never really take off. Take the Betamax video tape for example – beta what? (you're probably saying). People stop using a product or service when there aren't enough other users in the network to support its take-up. On the other hand, certain products appear ubiquitous. This issue became wholly apparent to me when the analysts where I work had to decide which statistical package to use.

There are various statistical packages that we economic analysts use to perform our data extracts or complex econometrics (applying economics to statistics). Each package has its pros and cons, and it's a matter of personal preference as to which package you like the most.

At some point, where I work, the analysts used the gamut of software available to them. Some years later, a clear frontrunner had emerged as the dominant software of choice for nearly all of the analysts. If all of the programs had their own individual merits, why had a single piece of software become the most popular?

The force at work was that the frontrunner software had reached a critical mass, which propelled its prolific use. Once it had a critical mass of users, it only made sense for new users to adopt this particular program to conduct their statistical work.

In my field, people send underlying data spread sheets in particular file formats that are only compatible with certain programs. Also, in this digital world we live in, analysts share their syntax files (a file containing computer code to carry out commands) in particular file types. This means you need a specific statistical package to access strings of computer code gold. Now, couple all of this with the costs associated with learning how to use a statistical package. This steers new users to only invest in the dominantly used package. Why would a new user invest his or her time in learning an obscure package that other users can't interact with? This is a bit analogous to choosing to learn a new language: Would you pick Latin, for example?

NB: Betamax is a type of videotape that some considered to be superior to VHS tapes, but it lost out on market influence partly due to critical mass problems. Consumer preferences and affordability also played a role. With advances in technology that have given us DVDs, both tape formats are now obsolete.

#16

Sigmoid curve

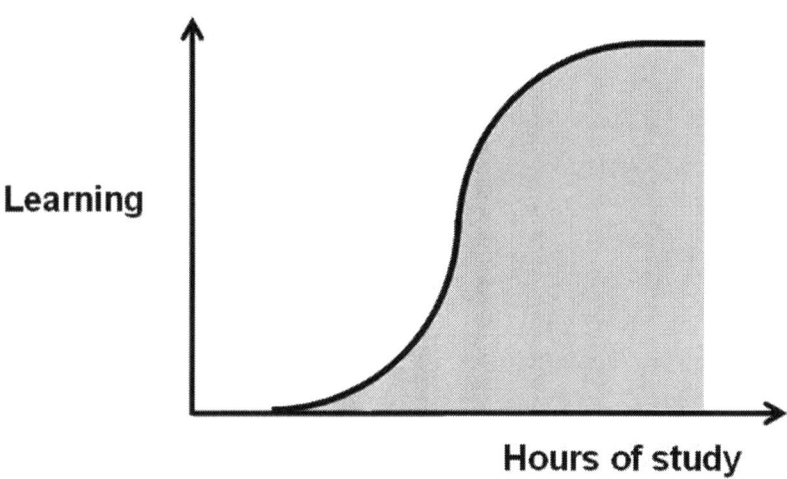

The rather strange-sounding Sigmoid curve refers to a mathematical function that when plotted, forms an S shape. There are a multitude of real-life events that match the shape of the Sigmoid curve. My example explains the highs and lows that I experienced when grappling to master secondary school mathematics.

In my final year of secondary school, I began Christmas break agonising over a predicted C grade. I was registered to sit the higher maths exam just six months later. My maths teacher gave me a load of GCSE books to kick-start my ascent to a higher grade.

I remember struggling with the first few pages of the book. The algebra may as well have been written in ancient Greek – I found it incomprehensible. During my Christmas break and into January, my hard work and perseverance slowly began to pay off. I learnt how to factorise, expand out brackets and use formulas.

By Easter, I sped through cancelling out terms and improved my trigonometry skills. I was making leaps and bounds in my mastery of maths. I was on a steep ascent up the learning curve.

With some newfound confidence, I started attending after-school maths clubs to fine-tune a few areas. I found that I was progressing in my knowledge, but at a much slower rate than before, the reason being that I had almost exhausted all the topics on the syllabus. Even with hours of additional practice and reading, I had already mastered the bulk of it. My learning of maths plotted against my hours of study fit the Sigmoid curve almost perfectly. I've observed this learning cycle with other secondary school children when I volunteer to teach them maths.

In case you're interested, my hard work paid off. In the summer following the end of secondary school, I opened up my results envelope to see a satisfying and well-deserved A grade staring back at me.

Returns to education

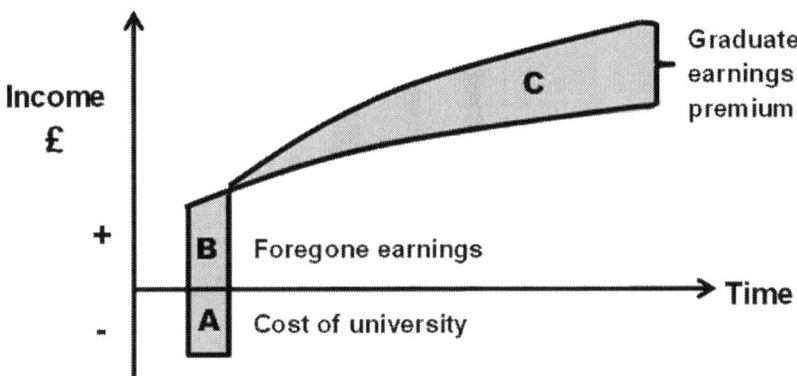

My university undergraduate days were amongst the best years of my life. I studied economics at Queen Mary University of London on Mile End Road. Apart from the university and independent cinema, the third most prominent feature of this road is a plethora of fried chicken shops. I must have devoured fried chicken at least four out of five days a week, excepting Fridays, when I'd treat myself to a döner kebab.

In spite of my fat-laden diet, I studied hard at university. I was the annoying student who constantly raised my hand in classes to answer the problem set questions. Our exam results would be posted on the departmental notice board, anonymised by student ID number. I often looked up my results by searching for the highest marks and then checking if it matched my student ID. After three hard years slogging away at study, I graduated from university, achieving the highest mark in my year. But what was the cost of going to university, and would it be worth it in the long haul? In economics, we tend to use cost–benefit analysis to make decisions. If the benefits exceed the costs, it's often worth taking a decision forward. In my university days, I encountered two main types of costs. First, the direct costs of buying books, notepads, stationery, etc. (section A). The government paid for my fees, as I qualified for a fee exemption. The second main costs I bore were foregone earnings. I worked at Marks & Spencer for 12 hours per week whilst at university. Given that I was studying, I couldn't work many more hours than this, let alone work full-time. I was giving up some potential earnings, and this can be treated as a cost (section B).

The time after graduation involves defining a counterfactual, that is, an alternative state of the world in which I receive the earnings profile of a college-leaver. Imagine, like in the film *Sliding Doors*, that I miss the train to university and end up in an alternate life where I enter the labour market after finishing college. Given widely accepted evidence, I would have earned a lower amount in wages if I didn't go to university. This is the graduate earnings premium and is treated as a benefit (section C). So was my decision to go to university worth it? I would say it was, as the benefits exceeded the costs.

I am sometimes curious what my alternative non-university life would have been like. At school, my ideal occupation was a bin man, so my *Sliding Doors* alternative may have involved working outdoors and driving a lorry – a very different world compared to my life as an economist.

#18

Purchasing power parity

Purchasing power parity

 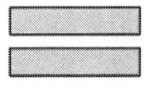   

Price of domestic good
in domestic currency

Price of foreign good
in domestic currency

After a 10-year-long dry spell of not travelling abroad during my twenties, I broke into my savings account and splashed out on two holidays in six months. The first was to Iceland during a bitter January chill. The other trip was to Japan in the summer, where I visited Buddhist temples and sampled the technology mayhem that is the Akihabara district in Tokyo.

Holidays are great life experiences; you get to expose yourself to different customs, sights and languages. The other thing that you quickly grasp is the necessity to quickly convert the local currency back into your currency, in my case, pound sterling. Not only did this give me a chance to practice my mental arithmetic, it also allowed me to compare the relative price of goods. When making such a comparison, I was factoring in the exchange rate and seeing if the price of the good differed. In other words, I was assessing my purchasing power.

Purchasing power parity occurs when the price of a same good is equal in two countries after adjusting for currency exchange rates. This can be illustrated by two instances in which I had to buy a baguette sandwich in Iceland and Japan. I choose this example because the baguettes involved were fairly similar. It's a type of good that doesn't vary much across the globe.

First, let's take Iceland: I purchased my baguette in Icelandic kronor. The exchange rate at the time was about 200 kronor to one British pound. At the time, I had just enjoyed a relaxing dip in the Blue Lagoon and wanted lunch. I grabbed my baguette from the display counter and almost fainted. My quick maths told me that the baguette cost about £7. That is extortionate – even for London prices in the heart of Mayfair, I'd struggle to find a standard baguette for that price. Clearly, I was not experiencing purchasing power parity.

I purchased the second baguette in Hiroshima in Japanese yen. What isn't very well known about Japan is that it has some of the best bakeries in the world. In this instance, I was killing time before catching a bullet train, so I bought a coffee, a baguette and a superb scone. After eyeballing the receipt, I calculated that the items on my tray cost a total of £5. In London, keeping the quality of the tray items constant, that would have set me back £8. Again, there wasn't parity of purchasing power, but at least I was gaining money instead of losing it.

The lesson I learned from all of this is to pack extra dried food in your suitcase if you're going to visit Iceland.

Lorenz curve

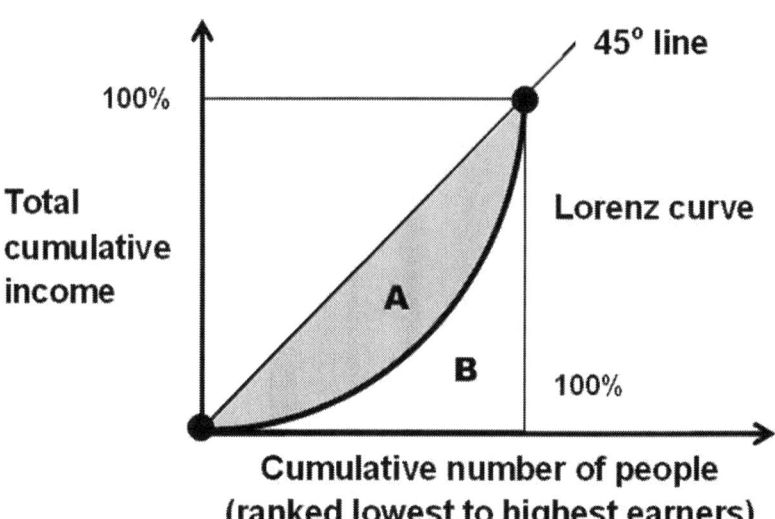

iving in London, I witness the inequality in wealth distribution on a daily basis. Walk around the City of London or Canary Wharf, and you can see high-paid individuals splashing around their wealth. Enter any retail shop, and someone earning minimum wage is probably serving you. During a walk, I was captivated by a story of struggle that a Scottish homeless person wrote out in pastels on the pavement in front of the National Gallery. He was asking for donations for his excellent pavement artwork, as he wanted to start a business. He even had a Twitter account so that people could follow his story. I haven't quite worked out how he gets broadband access to tweet, but I hope he's successful, as his artwork was mesmerising.

How can the uneven income distribution in London be represented on a graph? One way is to use the Lorenz curve. This curve first ranks everyone in terms of earnings from lowest to highest and then plots this on the x-axis. It then plots the cumulative total income on the y-axis. Given its design, the scale on both axes stops at 100%. What's clever about the Lorenz curve is that a 45° line drawn from the origin of the chart gives the line of equality. If London had an equal distribution of income (i.e. everyone had the same income), as you add up the cumulative income, this would run along the 45° line.

Cumulative income is represented by area B, while area A is a measure of inequality. The Gini coefficient is a number that can used to describe income inequality. The coefficient number lies between zero and one and is a fraction of areas A/(A+B). A higher Gini coefficient number indicates greater income inequality.

A report by the Joseph Rowntree Foundation in 2013 put London's Gini coefficient at around 0.34 – the highest of any city in Britain.

20

Increasing returns to scale

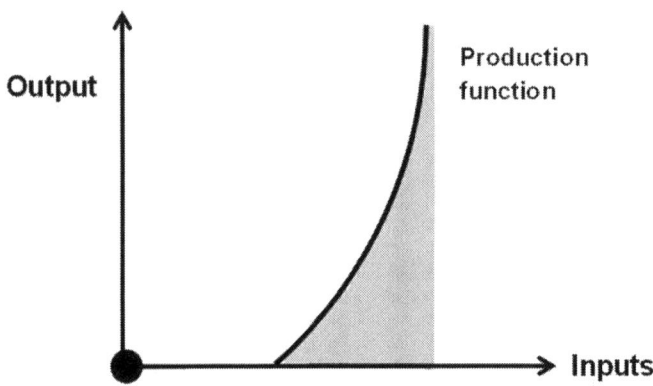

I n 2014, I attended a leadership course in Horsham, and what sticks in my mind was an exercise I performed involving paper cubes. What better way to practice leadership than a fictitious exercise in which you play the role of a small manufacturing company that produces cubes for a one-off order?

We started off in four groups of about five people each, all of whom were competing against each other to produce the highest tower of cubes we could make within 30 minutes. We each had a team leader and a production line of template makers, gluers and folders. I've never before heard a grown adult yell 'I can't glue'! The pressure clearly got to some people, and at the end of 30 minutes, each team had produced a small, sad pile of wonky paper cubes.

The course trainers allowed us to redeem ourselves the next day by repeating the exercise, but this time, all 20 of us would work as a super team. The inputs that we had available, our labour force, raw materials and tools such as scissors all quadrupled. If our inputs had quadrupled, would our output of cubes quadruple as well? What actually happened was that the number of cubes we produced increased by over tenfold. We had achieved increasing returns to scale; we had increased our output more than proportionally compared to the increase in inputs.

Our efforts were like a scene out of *Fantasia*, and like Mickey Mouse, our cubes seem to multiply by themselves. Clearly, we had no sorcery to draw on, so here's how we achieved an increasing returns to scale. To start with, we could better assign tasks to people based on their skill set. The best drawers made the cube templates, those who had a second calling as origami experts took to folding and those without a glue phobia got stuck pasting together the paper.

We also shared knowledge by offering the best production tips and designs for the cube template. The most valuable piece of advice was cutting multiple sheets of paper at once to churn out templates at a greater speed. Also, with a larger scale of production (and tools), we found there was less downtime for individuals, as we could flexibly move labour to where it was needed most.

We ended up with a massive pile of perfectly formed cubes on a table. The pile was so high, Mickey Mouse himself couldn't have done any better.

21

Heaviside step function

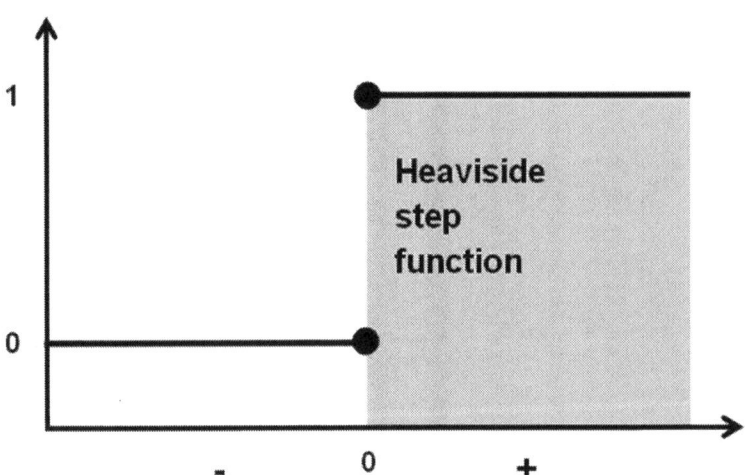

One of my best jobs was working at Marks & Spencer whilst I was a student. I worked at the Fenchurch Street branch, which is near a financial hub in East Central London. I was near many banks, and I ended up helping the investment bankers who came in calculate 15% off their sales items.

Working at Marks & Spencer was the first time I really interacted with people from a wide variety of ages, races and nationalities.

This job also gave me my first insight into management in a commercial setting. To this day, Marks & Spencer is the best employer I have ever had, and it's primarily down to its fantastic management practices. In this regard, it was way ahead of the curve, as simple things like team huddles to aid staff communication, relay information and raise morale were commonplace. My later employers would only cotton on to this tactic many years later.

I was also part of an employee voice panel and was elected to my post thanks to the votes of my menswear department teammates.

Our store in Fenchurch Street was a new branch. For a few months, most of the staff worked at different stores to train before assembling as the Fenchurch Street staff. A few months after opening, to mark the significant moment, the management wizards decided to invite us in small groups to their offices to eat a few snacks, and more importantly, drink 'Fenchurch Street fire punch'. I'm still not sure what was in that potent punch, but our morale and productivity skyrocketed after exiting the managers' offices.

This tale can be plotted using the rather scary-sounding Heaviside Step Function. This function resembles a step in which values below zero are given a constant zero value and values that are positive have a value of one. In my case, negative values on the x-axis of the chart represent the days pre-Fenchurch Street punch; the days after this introduction are positive values. I can plot the extra boost in team morale and productivity from drinking the punch on the y-axis. A step change in morale and productivity occurred after our meeting with the senior managers.

I should add that the cup of punch I had was crimson red in colour and non-alcoholic.

22

Bundling goods together

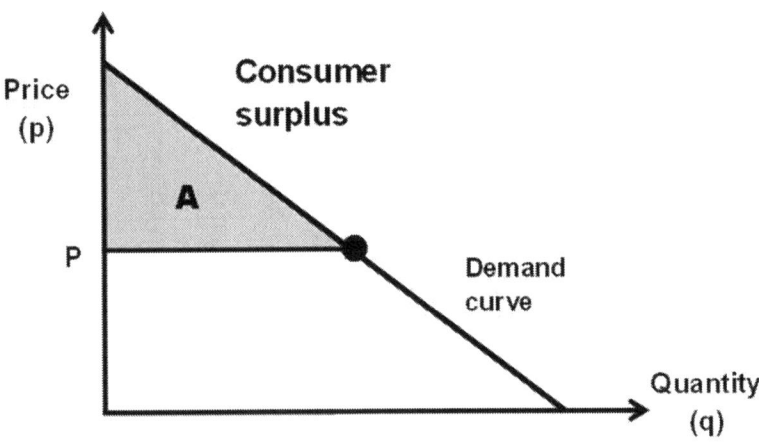

When I was eight, the shop Woolworths was still in existence and the top football league was called Division One. Since then, the 2008 financial crisis curtailed Woolworths' presence on the high street and the Premier League is now the best football league in England. Also, when I was eight, I used to spend my pocket money on Candy Sticks. I have no idea what the precise ingredients for Candy Sticks are, but I'm sure the sugar content approximates 100%. These white sticks resembled cigarettes and had a similarly addictive effect.

The reason my older brother and I bought these sweets was not because we wanted to have child-friendly cigarettes. The sweets were not even our favourite from the selection available at Woolworths. Our persistent purchase of Candy Sticks was due to the football player cards contained in every pack. We were determined to obtain the entire collection of football player cards. Week after week, we would devour countless amounts of Candy Sticks in pursuit of the rarest of the player cards.

How does this relate to economics? The sweet-maker had bundled two things together: the Candy Sticks sweets and the football playing cards. The effect on its young consumer base was to extract a greater proportion of consumer surplus from them.

Consumer surplus is the amount that consumers value the goods they buy over and above the price they pay. A demand curve in economics plots the price that a consumer is willing to pay in exchange for various quantities of that good. Typically, the demand curve is downward-sloping, as consumers demand less as the price increases. Consumer surplus is the area between the demand curve and the price paid (section A).

By making consumers buy goods that are bundled together, producers can extract a greater share of consumer surplus. My brother and I were willing to pay just so much for the Candy Stick sweets on their own, but by adding in the football playing cards, the sweet-maker could up the price and my quantity demand would remain unaffected (as I also placed value on the player cards).

We handed over copious amounts of our consumer surplus to the sweet-maker and still never found the rarest cards. My brother wrote to the sweet-maker asking for the five missing cards that we needed to complete our collection. To our surprise, the cards we needed actually arrived in the post.

23

Risk aversion

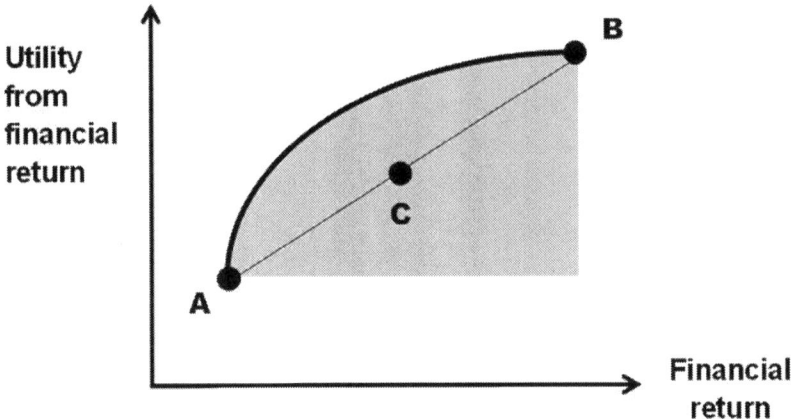

After endless overtures from my bank's financial adviser, I succumbed to an investment meeting with him. I had amassed a healthy amount of savings and was interested in making some interest beyond the almost zero per cent return offered by my regular savings account.

I've never been a massive risk-taker in life and would definitely describe myself as risk-averse when it comes to financial investments. Risk aversion can be represented by plotting the financial return on the x-axis against the utility achieved. As a quick reminder, utility represents the enjoyment I obtain. The shape of a risk-averse investor is a concave function (at primary school, my teacher would say that concave functions look like the entrance to a cave).

There are three investment options on the chart above. Product A gives a small financial return, product B gives a large return and product C gives a return that is the average of products A and B.

Given that I am risk-averse, if you gave me the option of a 100% guarantee of receiving the return of product C versus a more riskier financial product that on average gives the return of product C, I would prefer the option of a 100% guarantee of return over the riskier option. This is represented on the graph by the average utility of products A and B, which lies below the utility I would get from product C.

In hindsight, my chat with my financial advisor was not a fruitful one. After listening to him bang on about various financial products, I choose to invest £20,000 in a stocks and shares ISA (individual savings account). Two years later, I had a rather dismal £100 return to show for it.

24

Free riding

Person 2

Normal form of game

*Best response

		Work	Don't work
	Work	(-4,-4)	(-4,8*)
Person 1	**Don't work**	(8*,-4)	(0*,0*)

W orking on team projects can be very rewarding, but it can also be a complete nightmare. Looking back at university, it trained me for the world of work by devising group-based projects. The teacher would ask me to collaborate with my fellow classmates. On the whole, the people I went to university with were nice, well-rounded people. However, I was on an economics course, and these seemingly nice people began relying on their economic instincts. In a group project environment, this results in the problem of free riding.

Free riding in this context involves doing no work yourself and relying on the rest of the group to complete the project. Why does this occur? Two crucial conditions need to be present: first, the non-excludability condition. For some sadistic reason, even if you grassed up a slacker in your group to the lecturer, he or she would say it's your problem and wouldn't exclude them from the group mark.

If your fellow project teammates know this, they are unlikely to do much work if the rest of the group is working hard, as they will also get the group mark despite contributing little or not at all. The other vital condition is non-rivalry; in plainer English, this means that the use of the good or service by one person doesn't prevent others from benefiting from that good or service. In my case, because the slacker also got the group mark and benefited from it along with all of the other members, assigning a group mark to one person doesn't prevent others from accessing that benefit. In a nutshell, the non-rival condition was satisfied.

Two conditions met equal a perfect storm! My fellow teammates were either great economists or a lazy bunch of students, as they usually slacked off. I was a geek, so I always worked hard, and at times, produced the project entirely on my own, as I was the most interested in getting a good mark. This would further compound my woe, as a typical set of pay-offs for a free riding game would lead my slacker teammates not to contribute (their best response to me choosing to work hard).

Thank goodness in the world of real work, poor project team members can be reprimanded and the non-excludability and non-rival conditions can be broken!

25

Engel curve

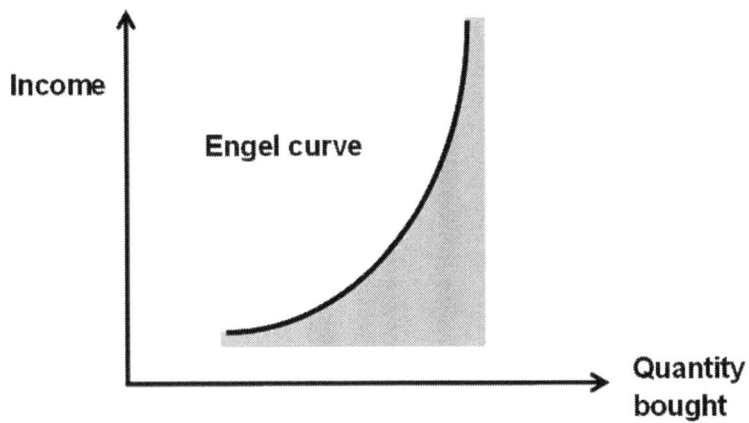

One of my addictions in life is coffee. The caffeine picks me up when I feel a bit sluggish, and I'm a bit like a kid in a sweet shop when visiting a cafe. There are so many delicacies to choose from, plus there are plenty of cakes to complement the cup of hot beverage.

Purchasing coffee from a coffee shop is usually an expensive affair, with extras like cinnamon and pumpkin flavouring boosting the price even further. When I joined the world of office work after graduating, I was a genuine penny pincher. I've already come clean about my daily £1.30 chips-and-beans diet at the time. In addition to this, I made the decision to never buy shop-made coffee. I brought a jar of instant coffee to work and brewed my own at home.

As the years passed, my salary increased (see #4: backward-bending supply labour curve for a reminder of my pay growth trajectory).

In tandem with my pay growth was the quantity of shop-made coffee I purchased. There was a distinct positive correlation between my salary growth and the increase in the amount of coffee I bought.

If I plot this on a graph, with my income on the y-axis and quantity bought on the x-axis, I come up with the Engel curve. If the Engel curve is upward-sloping, it means that as my income increases, the amount of coffee I buy increases. In economics, we call this type of good a 'normal good'.

If there are normal goods, are there also abnormal goods? Not quite, but there are 'inferior goods', in which the amount of the good demanded falls as your income increases. For me, my chips-and-beans lunch was an inferior good, as I ate this meal on a regular basis but weaned myself away from it as my salary increased. I now only eat chips and beans to reminisce about my impoverished days as a graduate employee.

26

Tragedy of the commons

Tragedy of the commons

often read the *Metro* newspaper, which once featured an article about the Save the Pangolin campaign. The slightly odd-looking animal above is the humble pangolin. The pangolin is a scaly fellow whose scales are made from keratin, the same protein that forms human hair and fingernails. Its natural habitat is in Africa and Asia. Its diet consists of ants and termites, and it occasionally has to fend off a lion or two. In addition to lions, the pangolin has to battle humans. Pangolins are hunted for their meat or scales, forcing this animal onto the endangered species list.

Why is the pangolin on the verge of extinction, and how can this be linked to economics? The case being presented here is a classic example of the 'tragedy of the commons'. The original tragedy of the commons refers to a situation in which individuals act with their own interests in mind, leading to an outcome that isn't best at the societal level. The commons is a reference to a common resource.

In the case presented here, the private benefits to a person would be the enjoyment he or she gets from hunting the poor pangolin, eating its meat and making products from its scales. The person would weigh up the costs of his or her hunting activities against the private benefits he or she gains. If a person were purchasing pangolin meat, he or she would assess the purchase price against the enjoyment he or she receives from eating pangolin meat. For these individuals, their private benefits (benefits that only they accrue) exceed the private-level costs (costs that only apply to them). Standard economic theory tells us that if the benefits exceed the costs, you should move forward with the decision.

What is missing from the analysis above is consideration of society as a whole. At the societal level, the benefits are pretty minimal, as the benefits fall on the small number of private individuals involved. The societal-level costs, however, are huge, as over-hunting of the pangolin will disrupt the natural ecosystem and will eventually lead to its extinction.

In tragedy of the commons type problems, individuals who are acting in their best interests tend to overuse the common resource, sometimes to the point of its complete depletion. Hopefully, with more societal-level thinking, the pangolin won't make the list that includes the dodo and the T. rex.

27

Satiation point

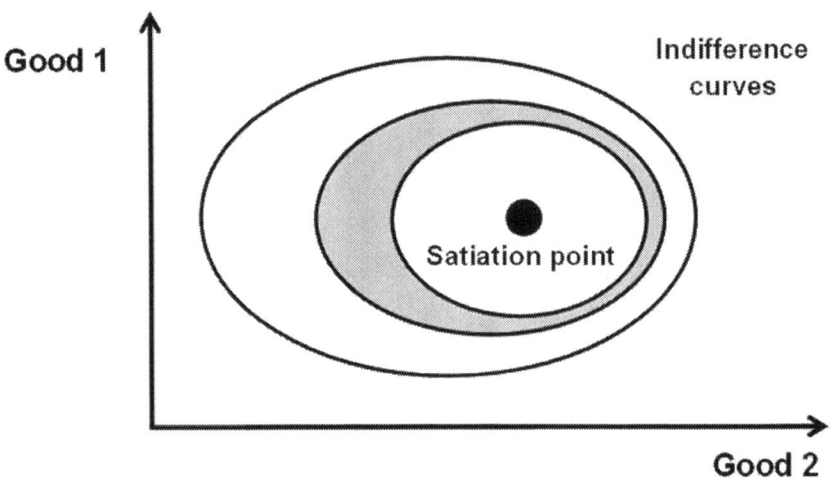

When I was a teenager, my brother and I created the all you can eat Pizza Hut Buffet Challenge. We would head down to Pizza Hut and eat as many pizza slices and plates of salad as our bellies could handle. We would keep a running total of our slice consumption by storing up a pile of crusts on an empty plate. A standard pizza is cut up into eight slices. We were racking up slice counts in excess of 16 each, in other words, more than two whole pizzas per teenage boy. I had a two-year age disadvantage over my brother, but I when it came to eating contests, we were locked in a dead heat for victory.

We would start our meal as soon as the buffet opened, which was shortly after noon. What ensued was a three-hour eating marathon that lasted until the buffet closed.

Our enjoyment at the start of the session was great. A little while into the eating challenge, we were still obtaining higher levels of enjoyment as we sampled all the types of pizza and salad on offer. Halfway through, we would hit an eating brick wall, and copious soft drinks were needed to continue. A normal adult at this point would say 'I've had enough' and declare satisfaction. Eating any more than this would bring on a bellyache and potential nausea.

The graph above depicts this very point, labelled the satiation point. The graph plots indifference curves in a contour style. Think of a map of a mountain, in which the rings indicate the height of the mountain. In the case of the graph, the rings indicate higher levels of enjoyment as you move inward toward the satiation point. Once at the satiation point, you have reached the optimal consumption of good one and two, in this case, pizza and salad. Any further consumption of either food would lead to your belly hurting and reduce your level of enjoyment, moving you to a lower indifference curve.

My brother and I tried to bankrupt Pizza Hut by literally eating as much as we could, consuming into the far upper right hand corner of the graph. My overeating would sometimes win me the eating contest against my brother, but it left me with a bloated and aching belly because I refused to give up at my satiation point.

28

Box plots

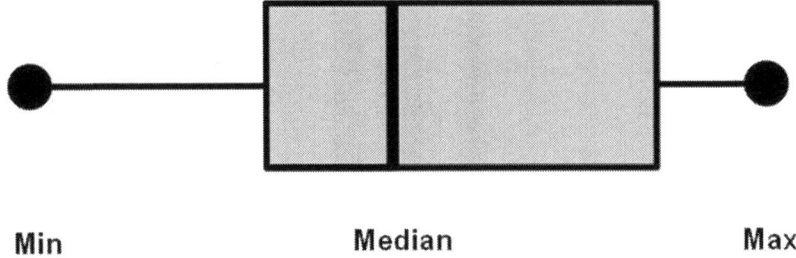

Min   Median   Max

Box plot

Box plots can be used to describe a whole assortment of data. In economics, they can be used to plot share price movements in a day, how earnings are dispersed in an economy or how varied a set of forecasts for output growth can be. My first introduction to box plots was not during my undergraduate economics course, but far earlier in my primary school days.

At my state-funded primary school, there were usually at least 30 children per class. I was short, very short. My father was 1.83 metres tall, and my older siblings towered over me, but for some reason, the tall gene passed me by.

A popular exercise we conducted in class would be to line up in height order to work out who was the tallest and where we all fit in. To further rub in how short I was, our teacher introduced us to a statistical tool called a box plot.

A box plot registers the smallest and largest value at each end – in this case, the shortest and tallest students in my class. A box is in between these two ends; its outer edges represent the height of the child who is taller than 25% of the rest of the class (the 25th percentile). The other outer edge of the box is the height of the child who is taller than 75% of the class (the 75th percentile). The median height – the lucky child who is taller than 50% of the class – is marked inside the box.

I was so vertically challenged, I remember being taller than only two other children. The saving grace was that at least I wasn't the shortest and at the start of the box plot. With 30 children in the class, that meant I was taller than 7% of the class. I'm not sure if it was down to drinking copious amounts of milk, but I grew to an adult height of 1.73 metres. This is acceptable, as it enables me to comfortably obtain items from the top kitchen cabinets and reach the handrails on trains.

29

Loss aversion

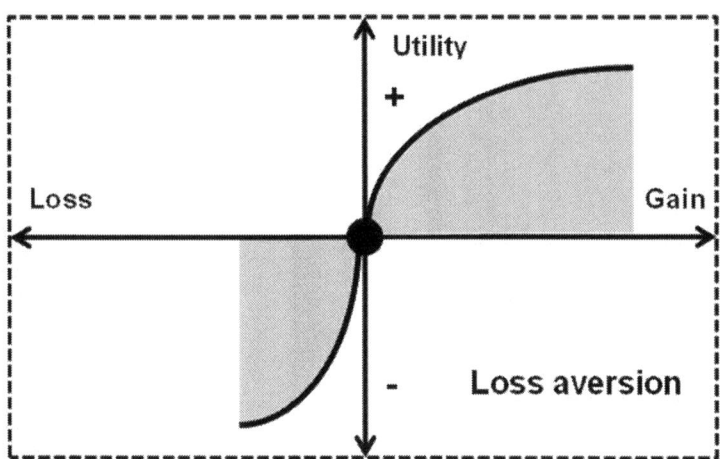

No one likes losing. The feeling of loss can be experienced with money, for example, losing a bet, or in sports, such as losing a game of football. When we lose, we often grow disappointed, and in economics, we call this disutility (i.e. negative utility). A win, on the other hand, brings on a rush of endorphins and loads of happiness (positive utility).

For a few years, I played in a five-a-side football league through work. It was a mixed league and its primary purpose was to be fun. Football matches would take place in an underground sports hall. The pitch was uniquely characterised by three concrete pillars that ran down the centre. I was a mercurial player, sometimes playing a great game and even scoring, and other times, making howling mistakes. Overall, my team wasn't very gifted, but on very rare occasions, I played on the side that won the match. To be more precise, I was on the winning side 5% of the time and on the losing side 95% of the time (I never drew a game).

On victorious days, the team would go down to the pub and celebrate with a well-earned drink. The whole squad would be on a high and have plenty of utility. I'm going to assign an illustrative level to this utility, let's say 50 from a three-goal win.

What was the level of disutility to squad members from a three-goal defeat? It's tempting to say minus 50 because we lost, so our utility is negative and a three-goal win has a 50 positive utility. In reality, our loss was much worse than minus 50 – I would say it was closer to minus 100. In the latter scenario, we would play the blame game that follows a post-match analysis, which pairs nicely with the humiliation and dejection suffered whilst losing.

In economics, there is a theory that the utility experienced from a gain is less than the disutility experienced from an equally sized loss. This theory is called loss aversion, and it was often present when I played football. I guess in non-economics talk, I truly am a sore loser.

30

Compound interest

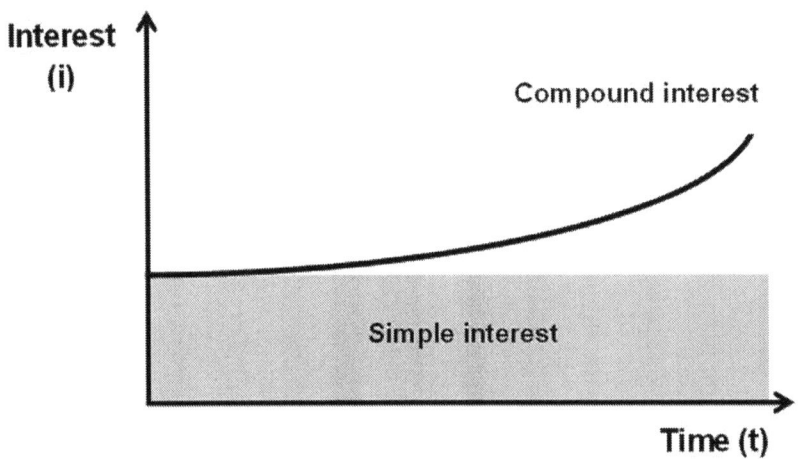

I am a notoriously diligent saver, as I'm a cheapskate when it comes to spending. If I can wear a jumper that has holes in it but still keeps me warm, why should I buy a new jumper? As well as tattered jumpers, I have a tendency to keep hold of my shoes. My current pair is five years old and is still going strong. I have even considered up-cycling them by buying new laces to extend their longevity.

As a result of this tight grasp on my purse strings, over many years, I have accumulated a very healthy bank balance. I always kept my savings in a single bank, but in 2008, I was forced to take drastic action.

Most of us still remember that 2008 was the year of the huge financial crash and the consequent economic recession. The government limits the amount of savings that it will protect if a financial institution goes bankrupt. With the risk of banks going under a real possibility, I decided to take swift action and immediately put some of my money in another bank. Savings are protected per bank account, so spreading my money out across multiple banks would mean that the government would protect and reimburse a greater amount if my banks failed.

I was in a rush and invested some of my money in a one-year bond. A bond is a financial product that pays an amount of interest at the end date of the bond (maturity date) along with the original amount invested (the principle). The type of bond that I invested in would be automatically reinvested for another year if I didn't withdraw the money at the maturity date. Interest rates were low after the recession, and I ended up leaving the money in the bond for seven years until I needed it to pay for a property.

After that seven-year period, I got back my original investment and loads of return in interest. The rate offered to me was very modest, so why was the return high? Each year, my starting balance to my bond would be the original investment plus the previous year's interest. That year's interest would be calculated on a higher starting balance. Every year, I earned interest on the previous year's interest payments. This compound interest grew with every passing year, and I'm grateful for it, as it funded the deposit for my flat.

NB: If I only earned interest on my original investment, the interest payment would have been the same each year (this is called simple interest).

31

Time preference

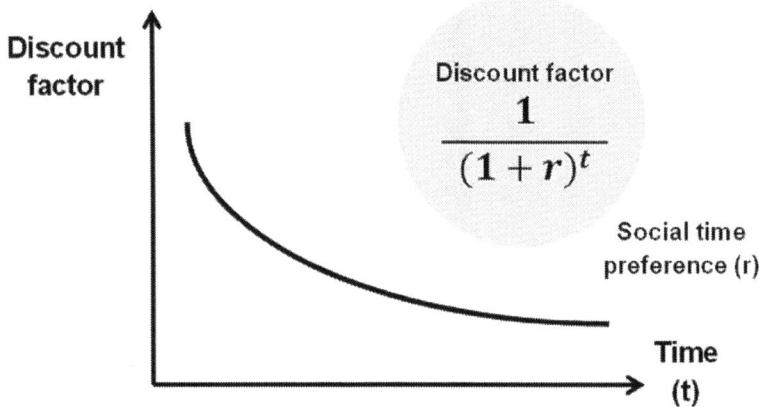

Discount factor

Discount factor

$$\frac{1}{(1+r)^t}$$

Social time preference (r)

Time (t)

Patience is a virtue; unfortunately, it's something I don't have. I hate waiting in queues in a shop, for exam results to come through or to receive money. Can economics be used to represent my impatience? Yes it can, and it seems that I'm not alone in this trait.

There is an accepted theory that if you offer someone £100 to-day or £100 in a month's time, most people would prefer the £100 today. The primary reason for this is that individuals place a value on waiting for money. So, if the amount on offer is the same (£100), it will be worth less in one month's time compared to receiving it today. Just imagine if the period were one year – the value of the £100 received in a year's time would be worth much less than receiving £100 today.

In the public sector world, there is a famous book called The Green Book. It argues that people's social time preference is 3.5%. In plain terms, this means that because of waiting, the value of a monetary amount received in one year's time must be 3.5% more compared to receiving the money today (to make the person indifferent). If you have to wait one more year, the value must rise by another 3.5%, and so on to maintain indifference.

On the above graph, the discount factor represents the value of the money received in the future compared to today. The further in the future the money is received, the less value we place on it today. In mathematics, we would say that this curve is asymptotically approaching the x-axis. In English, the curve is getting closer to the x-axis as the future point of receiving the money gets further away.

Here's an irksome personal example of social time preference. Once, I leant my friend Steve a fiver so that he could buy his lunch. Steve said he would pay me back soon – a day went by, a week went by, a month went by, and sometime after that, he paid me back. I had actually forgotten that he even owed me money and was willing to write it off. He made me wait for so long, its value to me was almost zero compared to the day I leant him the fiver!

#32

Passing along a tax

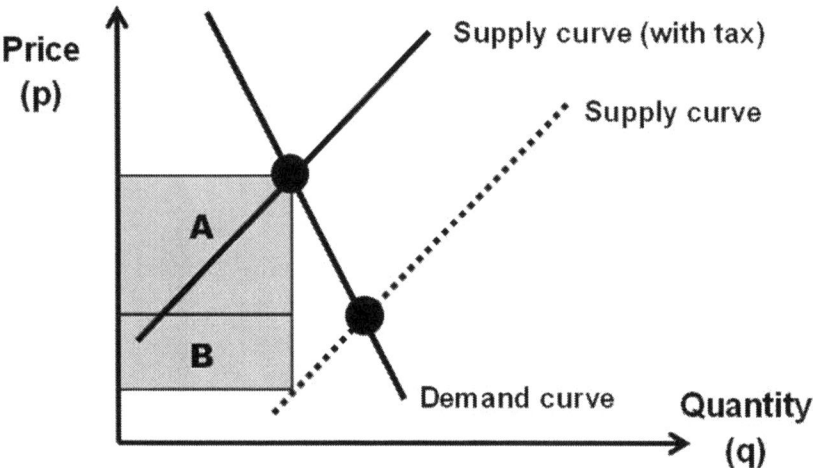

My canteen used to offer delectable hot meals at a reasonable price. Much better than the anaemic school dinners of my childhood, these meals included curries, vegetable tempura, jerk chicken and many more. That is, until the government raised the value added tax (VAT) by 2.5%. To my dismay, the canteen prices increased by something in the ballpark of 3%. Was it right that the entire tax increase should fall on its patrons?

Where I worked, I had access to outside dining options – food purchased elsewhere could still be consumed in the canteen.

Despite this, the canteen wielded significant power over us. When I had a busy meeting schedule, the canteen proved more convenient. Also, if it was raining, I preferred not to venture out just to find sustenance. The demand for canteen food was fairly inelastic; in other words, the canteen could raise prices a lot and our demand would fall only a little. This demand curve had a steep slope.

With that in mind, the canteen knew it could pass on the bulk of the VAT-related price rise to its customers. But why did the prices rise more than the aforementioned 2.5%? I believe the canteen rounded up to the nearest penny: my coffee now cost £1.29 (it originally was priced at £1.25, an increase of 3.2%), or the person calculating the price rise may have been bad at maths.

The above chart shows how the tax moves the supply curve upward. The price charged to the customers increases. Shaded area A represents the burden of the higher tax placed on the customers. The tax burden that the canteen (or more generally, the suppliers) experience is represented by shaded area B. In my case, shaded area B is equal to zero (the entire price rise was passed onto the customers). This would occur if the demand curve were vertical.

The actual demand curve was close to being vertical, so the canteen got away with passing along the tax to its loyal customers.

33

Herfindahl–Hirschman Index

$$HHI = \sum_{i=1}^{n} s_i^2$$

Herfindahl–Hirschman Index

I once lived on Brick Lane in London famous for its curry houses. The street was peppered with restaurant after restaurant, and you couldn't walk a few metres without waiters offering free poppadum as they trolled for customers. The food was good, made clear by the robust rodent population. The mice often made their way up from the restaurants to the flats above to sample the local residents' cooking as well.

Economic theory tells us that if there are a lot of competitors, there should be a lot of competition. But how is competition measured? There are a few measures out there, such as how much prices are above costs (an indicator of profit) or counting the number of firms in a market. But my favourite measure, perhaps just for how it sounds, is the Herfindahl–Hirschman Index (HHI). The HHI examines how concentrated an industry is. It measures the scale to which there are just a few firms with a large market share or many firms that each have small market shares.

The daunting equation for the HHI shown above adds up all the market shares of the restaurants after squaring them. If it summed up the market shares without squaring them first, the sum, by definition, would be 100%. Market share can be measured by a restaurant's share of the total street sales. In the most extreme case, if there was strong competition with loads and loads of restaurants, each of their shares would approach zero, as would the HHI. In the other extreme, if there was only one restaurant (poor competition), it would have a 100% share, and the HHI would be 10,000 (100^2). Over a period of about four decades, new restaurants continually sprang up on that street, but this growth has recently dwindled.

I don't have the necessary data to work out the precise HHI for all of the curry houses on that street, but some rough calculations based on around 30 restaurants having an equal share would put the HHI at just over 300. If for some reason, 10 restaurants closed, leaving only 20 restaurants, and they had equal market shares, would the HHI change? The answer is that it would, as the HHI responds to the amount of shares per restaurant and the total number of restaurants. Intuition tells us that fewer restaurants should lead to a fall in competition and an increase in the HHI. This is exactly what happens, as 20 restaurants with equal shares leads to an HHI of 500.

I personally wouldn't mind if there were fewer restaurants, as it would allow for more diversity in the street and create opportunities for one of my longest-held dreams: a cereal bar.

#34

Revealed preference

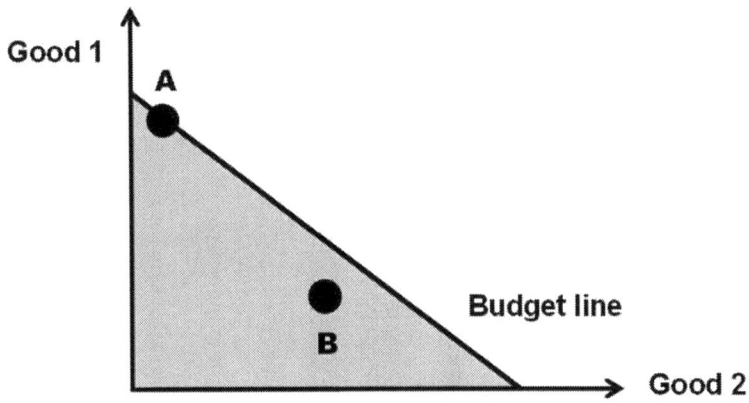

I get a glimpse of my colleagues' food preferences by observing what they purchase for lunch. For example, I hate goat's cheese and blue cheeses. This is rooted in a traumatic experience in which my sister once made me horrible Stilton-laced sandwiches when I was at school.

Lunchtimes at work can be very telling about a person's likes and dislikes when it comes to food. There are the super-healthy salad crunchers, the unhealthy fast food junkies, the vegetarians, etc. In economics, people's preferences are revealed after they make a purchase (this principle is called revealed preference). This is very different to stated preference, which is based solely on asking an individual for his or her view. The main flaw with stated preference is that people have a tendency to say what they think others want to hear as opposed to what they actually want. This certainly happens when I lie to my dentist about the amount of sugar that I eat.

Revealed preference can be plotted on a graph by first plotting the budget constraint. Let's take a simple example in which I can eat my favourite sugary snacks for lunch or a carrot and lettuce salad. If I call sugary snacks good one, the point on the y-axis is the maximum amount of snacks that I can buy if I spend my entire lunch money budget on snacks. Salad is good two, and the point on the x-axis is the maximum amount of salad that I can buy again through exhausting my entire lunch budget. The points on the budget constraint line show all of the financially affordable combinations of snacks and salad I can have whilst spending my entire budget. The area under the budget line represents all of the combinations of snacks and salads that don't involve spending my entire budget.

Actions definitely speak louder than words, as I hardly ever buy salad despite being able to afford it. My revealed preference is undeniably at point A on the graph, as nearly all of my money goes toward snacks or unhealthy lunch options as opposed to anything remotely resembling a balanced meal.

35

Negative externality

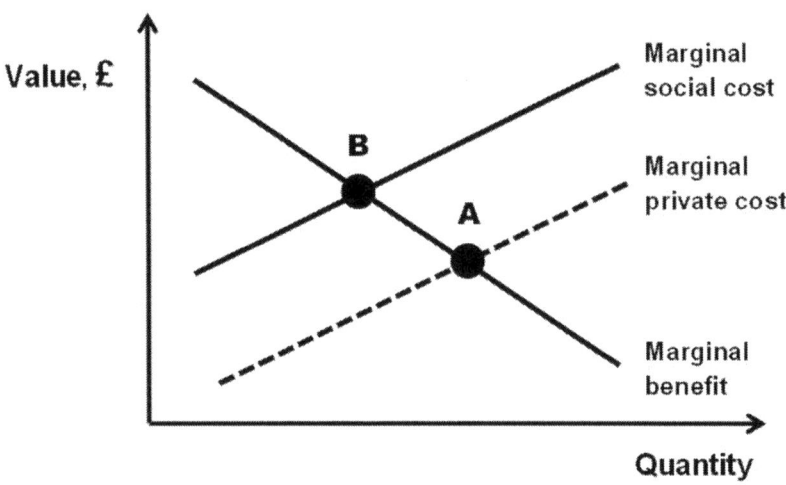

Value, £

Marginal social cost

B

Marginal private cost

A

Marginal benefit

Quantity

Travelling on the London underground can be a grotesque experience. In rush hour, you are squeezed into carriages where the concept of personal space seems never to have existed. There are the stretchers, who feel it necessary to use the arm rests such that they touch the commuters on the adjacent seats (otherwise, they feel they aren't sufficiently loosened up). But it's not the above that annoys me most when travelling on the Tube – it's people playing deafeningly loud music. Despite having earphones on, these people turn the volume up so high that even the train driver at the front of the train is privy to their music tastes.

Not only do these people usually have terrible auditory affinities, it's not pleasant for the rest of the carriage, who may prefer the company of their own thoughts. In economics, when one person's actions have a negative impact on others, it is known as negative externality.

The above graph plots a negative externality derived from the Tube example. The commuters who decide to play loud music are treated as private individuals. The cost of playing the music borne by them (download costs and battery power costs) is labelled 'private marginal costs'. These costs increase with the more music they play (a quantity increase). If the private individual is the only person we consider, he or she should play a quantity of loud music where the marginal benefit equals the marginal cost (point A).

There are, however, other commuters in the carriage (the society). The marginal social costs include everyone getting annoyed, and in extreme cases, suffering hearing damage or other stress-related diseases. The marginal social cost is an upward-sloping line, as these costs increase as the quantity of loud music increases. There are hardly any benefits to the rest of the carriage – nearly all of the benefits fall on the person playing the music. If the music player considers his or her impact on the rest of the carriage, he or she would play a lesser amount of loud music (point B). Point B is where the marginal social cost (the cost of playing one minute more of loud music) equals the marginal benefit to the person with the headphones.

When considering the negative externality on the wider carriage, the optimal amount of loud music played is less compared to the amount played when the private individual considers only him or herself. There is also an alternative view to this issue: the inconsiderate person with the roaring music could just lower the volume.

16183611R00047

Printed in Great Britain
by Amazon